Little Stevie Wonder

by Quincy Troupe

illustrated by

Lisa Cohen

HOUGHTON MIFFLIN COMPANY
BOSTON 2005

www.houghtonmifflinbooks.com

The text of this book is set in Triplex and Egbert.
The illustrations are acrylic on paper.

Library of Congress Cataloging-in-Publication Data

Troupe, Quincy.
Little Stevie Wonder / by Quincy Troupe ; illustrated by Lisa Cohen.
p. cm.
Summary: A poem tribute to blind musician and composer Stevie Wonder.
ISBN 0-618-34060-2
1. Wonder, Stevie—Juvenile poetry. 2. Rock musicians—Juvenile poetry. 3.
Blind musicians—Juvenile poetry. 4. African American musicians—
Juvenile poetry. 5. Children's poetry, American. [1. Wonder, Stevie—
Poetry. 2. Musicians—Poetry. 3. People with disabilities—Poetry. 4.
Blind—Poetry. 5. American poetry.] I. Cohen, Lisa, 1963- II. Title.
PS3570.R63L58
811'.54—dc22
2003017703

ISBN-13: 978-0618-34060-6
Book design by Sue Dennen

Manufactured in China
SCP 10 9 8 7 6 5 4 3 2 1

To my grandchildren: Amina
Grace, Zora, Andre, Lillian, Samuel,
and Trezhure—with deep love.
—Q. T.

For Mischa and Sally.
Shake, shake it, Wena!

Isn't he lovely,
this blind black boy
born to love everyone?

Oh yeah, isn't he lovely,
this small blind boy, thinking of his fingertips?
Snapping those fingers before unseeing eyes,
he starts humming.
Then he turns that humming into a song.
Shake it, shake, shake a tail feather, baby.

He shakes his head in time with the music,
shakes it from side to side —
makes up a beat and keeps the beat going
inside his mind, where he sees everything in
pictures.

Oh, isn't he lovely,
this blind black boy,
born to love everyone?
Isn't he lovely,
oh, isn't he lovely?

He was born on May 13, 1950, in Saginaw, Michigan, to Lula Mae Hardaway and Calvin Judkins, who name him Stevland Judkins. When Lula moves to Detroit, she carries little Stevland and he takes on a name from Lula's side of the family, Stevland Judkins Morris Hardaway.

Little Stevland grows up like a vibrating root listening to blues music on the radio.

He is a magical boy, this blind little boy.
What he can't see, he knows through touch,
through his seeing-eye fingertips,
through his big, warm heart
that thumps in time with the music
like an old African drum.

This young boy's heart is touched through love.
Love that turns into music.
Love that becomes
sweet-smelling flowers
blooming fresh in springtime,
after warm rain
has washed down.

And through his **ears** he sees more clearly than most people do with their **eyes.**

Oh, isn't he lovely,
this blind black boy
born to love everyone?
Isn't he lovely,
oh, isn't he lovely?

He is a fun-loving boy
who loves to play jump rope,
hide-and-go-seek,
And ring-around-the-rosy.

He is a curious boy, who imitates all the black singers he hears over the airwaves.

He starts banging on bongo drums when he is seven.

Starts playing the piano of the lady next door like he owns it when he is nine.

That's when everybody knows Little Stevie is a musical genius.

Then his uncle gives him a harmonica
and he starts singing in the choir.

Oh, isn't he lovely,
this blind black boy born to love everyone,
who feels and knows everything
through his fingertips and ears?

Genius boy who sees through sound
a toy car that drops on the hard floor,
a **quarter,** a **pin,** a **baseball,**
a **dime** that falls on the countertop.

Stevland Judkins Morris Hardaway,
whose head lives in dreams,
is always making up songs inside a rich
imagination.

And when the boy named Stevie starts singing in Detroit's back alleys and on crowded street corners, people cheer, clap their hands, and whistle.

Then one day a **"big man"** over at Motown, "Hitsville USA,"
hears Stevie sing, signs him to a record contract, and
gives him a new name:

Little Stevie Wonder.

When he is thirteen years old, Little Stevie
records a hit song called **"Fingertips."**

Then millions of people all over the world
dance the nights away
when they hear Little Stevie sing:

Soon Stevie becomes a song,
growing in the ears of people everywhere.
Fans snap and pop their fingertips
when they hear the Wonderman's music.
They smile and sway when
his hands caress his harmonica,
his fingertips and breath pulling sweet music—
    like magic—
from that old blues instrument of
    wood and polished steel.

Isn't he lovely,
Little Stevie Wonder,
born to love everyone?

In MUSIC OF MY MIND,
this beautiful voice
who sings like an angel on TALKING BOOK,
right before our eyes takes us to a "Higher Ground"
singing "Master Blaster (Jammin')" and

"Happy Birthday" for Martin Luther King, Jr.

Isn't he lovely
when he sings "Ribbon
in the Sky,"
this **Wonderman**
born to love everyone?

"Through thick and thin,"
he grows strong
and he

sings

and

sings.

Little Stevie grows into
a sequoia tree of a man.
He takes his INNERVISION,
his **words**,
his **voice**,
and spreads joy and peace,
telling everyone
that "We Are the World"
and harmonizing "Ebony and Ivory."

He keeps growing with a smile bright
as a clear daybreak on his dark, luminous face,
the **words of his songs now dazzling stars**,
shining diamonds in the night sky,
like words of Braille his fingers touch.

Isn't he lovely,
Stevland Judkins Morris Hardaway,
"Little Stevie Wonderland,"
Now Stevie Wonder?

Oh, isn't he lovely,
this luminous wonder of a man?
A sequoia tree of a man,
a rainbow of song,
born to love everyone!

Author's Note

Stevland Judkins Morris Hardaway was born on May 13, 1950, in Saginaw, Michigan, to Lula Mae Hardaway. Stevie's father was present at his son's birth but was not around while Stevie was growing up.

Stevie was born prematurely and put in a hospital incubator to help him breathe. But the oxygen in the incubator caused blindness. Doctors have since learned more about this problem and now protect the eyes of infants who need to be in an incubator after birth.

Blindness didn't hold Stevie back. His mother and brothers watched out for him but let him be a regular kid. His family and neighbors recognized Stevie's musical talent when he was very young.

Stevie's big break came when one of his best friends, Gerald White, convinced his brother, Ronnie, who sang with the Miracles, to listen to Stevie sing. Ronnie White couldn't believe Stevie's voice. He introduced Stevie to a talent scout at the Detroit offices of Motown, a new record company that was changing the music world. The scout quickly brought Stevie to Berry Gordy, the head of Motown. When Gordy heard Stevie on the harmonica and drums and piano, he knew Stevie was something special. Stevie signed a contract with Motown when he was ten years old and was given the performing name "Little Stevie Wonder."

When Stevie began recording and performing in Motown revues, he did his schoolwork with a tutor who traveled with him and watched over him at home and on the road.

In 1963, Stevie had his first big hit — "Fingertips, Part 2," a live recording from a Motown revue. It was the first live concert recording ever to go to number one on the pop music charts. Soon after, Stevie's album *Little Stevie Wonder: The 12-Year-Old Genius* rose to number one on the pop charts. Stevie went on to release singles and albums that have won nineteen Grammy Awards and an Oscar.

For more than four decades, Stevie Wonder has been a musical innovator, mixing styles and sounds and experimenting with electronic instruments before they were widely used. He has also been politically and socially active — speaking out for world peace and racial harmony; raising awareness about world hunger, AIDS, and homelessness; and supporting anti-drug and anti-drunk-driving causes and people with disabilities.

Stevie Wonder's music is everywhere — on the radio and television, in movies, and in his influence on other musicians. His way of seeing the world — through joy and peace — touches everyone.

Chronology

May 13, 1950	Stevland Judkins Morris Hardaway is born in Saginaw, Michigan
1954	Moves with his family to Detroit
1961	Signs a recording contract with Motown
1963	Hits number one on the pop music charts with "Fingertips, Part 2" and with LITTLE STEVIE WONDER: THE 12-YEAR-OLD GENIUS
1964	Drops "Little" from his professional name
1968	Graduates high school from the Michigan School for the Blind
1970	Marries Syreeta Wright, a Motown singer-songwriter
1971	Wins his first Grammy for SIGNED, SEALED AND DELIVERED; negotiates a new contract with Motown that gives him artistic control of his music; forms his own recording and production companies, Taurus Productions and Black Bull Music
1972	Divorces Syreeta Wright
1973	Suffers a near-fatal car accident that puts him in a coma for one day
1974	Wins three Grammy Awards for his album INNERVISIONS; a son, Mumtaz, is born
1975	Wins four Grammy Awards for FULFILLINGNESS' FIRST FINALE; writes "Isn't She Lovely" about the birth of his daughter, Aisha
1976	A son, Keita, is born
1980	Records "Happy Birthday" in honor of Martin Luther King, Jr., and begins advocating a national holiday to commemorate King's birthday (it's first celebrated in 1986)
1982	Performs at the "Peace Sunday" antinuclear rally at the Rose Bowl with Bob Dylan and Jackson Browne
1985	Participates in recording "We Are the World" with USA for Africa; wins an Oscar for Best Song, "I Just Called to Say I Love You," from *The Woman in Red,* and dedicates the award to Nelson Mandela, which gets his music banned in South Africa
1989	Inducted into the Rock and Roll Hall of Fame
1996	Receives a Lifetime Achievement Grammy Award
1997	Establishes the Vision Awards to recognize and promote technological breakthroughs that enhance the lives of people with disabilities
1999	Aisha has a son, Stevie Wonder's first grandchild; Wonder becomes the youngest recipient of a Kennedy Center Honor
2001	Performs at a benefit concert for the victims of the World Trade Center attack
2003	Receives a tribute to his music from other musicians on CONCEPTION: AN INTERPRETATION OF STEVIE WONDER'S SONGS

Select Discography

1963   The 12-Year-Old Genius

1966   Uptight (Everything's Alright)

1967   I Was Made to Love Her

1968   For Once in My Life

1972   Music of My Mind

1972   Talking Book

1973   Innervisions

1976   Songs in the Key of Life

1980   Hotter Than July

1982   Stevie Wonder's Original Musiquarium

All recordings on Motown label